Dr Abide Zenenga is an experienced educationalist with over 25 years of working with young people with autism (14–19). He is a father to a young person with autism himself and has interest in advancing the educational opportunities of young people with SEN. After obtaining a PhD at the University of Northampton in Special Educational Needs, Dr Zenenga founded Riverside Education in 2015, with the aim of supporting parents with autistic children. Dr Zenenga believes that as a Christian, he is called upon by God to share his story and to help families who have children with autism.

To our son Kupa, born with Down's Syndrome and autism. You give us so much joy and provide us with positive learning opportunities every day. You are our gift from God.

Dr Abide Zenenga

THE GIFT

AUSTIN MACAULEY PUBLISHERS™

LONDON • CAMBRIDGE • NEW YORK • SHARJAH

A CIP catalogue record for this title is available from the British Library.

ISBN 9781398438248 (Paperback)
ISBN 9781398438255 (ePub e-book)

www.austinmacauley.com

First Published 2022
Austin Macauley Publishers Ltd®
1 Canada Square
Canary Wharf
London
E14 5AA

I strongly believe that 'no man is an island'. So many people have made this book a reality. I am sincerely grateful to my two sons (Kupa and Kudzy) and my wife, Molline Grace Zenenga, who agreed to be part of this story and has always supported me in my darkest moments. Molly has been a pillar of strength in all of our prayer battles. I am also grateful to my friend Sade-Antonio-Patterson who helped me to write this book, and also to my business partner and friend Tony Copeland who has mentored and supported me into the business world. My family in Zimbabwe have never doubted this book and the Riverside Education staff who have become more than just work-colleagues but my family too. Last but not least, I am grateful to God, the Almighty, who has moved mountains for me and performed miracles before my own eyes. Amen.

Table of Contents

I strongly believe that all the gifts that we have come from God. I also believe that God will hold us accountable for not making use of these gifts to bless others. Everything we have is a gift from God. All good things are gifts from God (1 Timothy 6:17). This book is about the gift that myself and my wife have received in such unexpected circumstances. I have decided to share how we are using our gift to bless others who are less fortunate. Before you even begin to read our story, believe that God is writing your story and the same God who has done it for us, can and will do it for you too.

Although you may not know what your future holds, be assured that it is God who is holding your future. Many have already counted you out, so you try and talk yourself out of the visions and blessings which God has predestined for you. God blessed Moses, Joseph and Jacob in such magnificent ways. Even me, despite feeling unworthy, God has gifted me with countless blessings. He can bless you too because our status doesn't limit God; not even our own limitations can limit Him.

What a mighty God we serve. He sees our beginning and our end. We can only see our present. Let's be honest, many a times our past experiences distort our future expectations. Our God sees around corners but we can only see to the corners. We only see our past and have a limited perspective of our present but we serve a God who sees our future and is beckoning us to walk into it boldly. We feel unworthy and ill-equipped but even in our weaknesses; God will equip us, as he did with Moses. This mighty God uses ordinary people to do extraordinary things. Let Him use you too.

If God has given you a vision for a business, chase the dream and the vision, financial blessings will come as a consequence of your passionate pursuit of the vision. Seek ye the kingdom first and the rest shall be given (Matthew 6 vs 33). Whilst on your mission, God will continue to give you more challenges but He will equip you to win and overcome every single one of them. I'm reminded of Jesus who was constantly tempted and questioned. These challenges are just opportunities to develop you.

Whilst on your mission, be discerning of those around you, God will send encouragers, visionaries and people who have the same passion as you to propel you into the vision. Know who you have around you to help and heal you and those whose purpose is to hinder and hold you.

Also, do not be deceived: we don't own this wealth; we are just mere custodians of it. Let the light of God within us shine without (externally) so that what God blesses us with is a blessing to others too. Let others see and experience the glory of God within us. You are the salt of the earth (Matthew 5 vs 13), created to add 'taste' to the world in your own way. You were fearfully and wonderfully made (psalm 139 vs 14). There is only one you.

1. The History

My name is Abide Zenenga. I was born in rural Zimbabwe into a family of seven children. Although both of my parents didn't work, the family survived on farming. Selling the produce from our land was what enabled my parents to send all of us to school. As there were so many of us, the produce from the land was not enough to educate us and it took my parents selling almost the entire herd of cattle so that our schooling was paid for. Education was very important to them.

Just as many Zimbabweans, my parents knew that the only way out of poverty was education so schooling was not an option but essential for all of us. Admittedly, being the youngest boy in my family, I grew under the shadow of my siblings and I looked up to them a lot. I was considered to be an average student at school; I wasn't outstanding in any area of the curriculum like my brothers and sisters were and I did not expect much from myself. I don't think anyone expected much too.

Upon reflection, I was very much the 'David' of the household but when you are happy and satisfied with what you have, you will never grasp how pitiable you actually are. David was deemed just a shepherd boy by many around him.

He was the youngest too. Not much was expected of him, either. However, over two thousand years after his death, he is remembered for his courage, communion and contrition, in the book of the Bible entitled Psalm. David's story inspires me every day.

In the Bible, we learn that God spoke to the prophet Samuel, after He had rejected Saul (the previous king of Israel). God told Samuel that He had chosen a new king who was the son of Jesse. (1 Samuel 16:1). Interestingly, God never gave Samuel any further descriptions of the king whom He had chosen for himself. This has taught me that sometimes God withholds information from us because sometimes our own beliefs will distort our destiny?

This new king was one whom God had chosen for himself, not necessarily the people. This reinforces the reality that often people choose who they want, for their glory and their appeasement but as God chose David, God chose me. In all that has happened in my life, I was not the people's choice but God's choice, before the foundations of the earth (Ephesians 1:4).

This picture tells my story in full from the little boy I was to becoming the doctor I was destined to be.

During the time of the appointment, Jesse presented all of his sons as instructed; actually, all but one. David was the youngest; he was just the shepherd boy so he was not invited. I'm not sure whether he was overlooked, maybe just under looked. When Samuel saw Eliab, one of Jesse's sons, Samuel thought that he looked like the Lord's anointed so presumed Eliab was the one whom God wanted him to anoint. Instead, God warned,

"Do not look at his appearance or at his physical stature because I have refused him." (1 Samuel 16:7a.)

So often, we hold the misconception that to be the blessing and to receive the blessing, we have to look a physical way or have certain commodities. As humans, we look at what we have or what we don't have; God is not like us, He looks at our hearts (1 Samuel 16:7b). After all, David was the youngest son of Jesse. He was just a shepherd boy. This was his past and some aspects of his present. God, being Alpha and Omega, sees the beginning and the end. He makes no mistakes. He knows our present, He knows our potential, He also knows His perfect will for us.

Even Jesse never knew who he had raised or who he had in his house. He did not see nor discern the power which his youngest son possessed. At this event, which was purposed to anoint the divinely appointed king, the one who God had chosen, Jesse presented his sons. As Samuel looked with conviction at Jesse's sons, assured each was the one, God continued to tell him that He had refused them. Samuel was perplexed. He knew he heard God. He knew God told him that His chosen one was one of Jesse's sons: one of Jesse's sons were to be anointed.

However, with each son presented, seven to be exact, God said no! When Samuel called for the other son, David, the youngest, ruddy-looking one, the shepherd boy was presented. To everyone's amazement, God confirmed that this was the one whom he had chosen (1 Samuel 16:12) so Samuel anointed him.

Those who are not familiar with this bible story may relate and understand something almost similar that happened on a British TV show called 'Britain's Got Talent.' An unassuming lady called Susan Boyle came up the stage and everyone didn't expect much of her until she opened her mouth to sing. She sang beautifully and became an instant star. To date she continues to inspire other people through her music but to me, it's her story that struck me most. She became a music gift to the world when no one expected anything from her.

Back to my story, this was God's gift to David, to become king. David was also God's gift to the people. Even though I did not expect it, I now realise that God has made me a gift to some people. He has also gifted me with a great gift. As you read my story, I pray that it resonates with you and you realise that God doesn't make mistakes – ever. Even that which seems like it possesses the potential to render you powerless, our powerful God can use it to reveal His promises to you.

When I was growing up my mum asked me what I wanted to become and I said a doctor. From then on, she decided to call me doc but other people changed it to dok shortcut for dokororo (a word in our language that means chicken manure). Throughout my childhood I was known as Dokororo though my mum insisted on doc. This was meant to put me down and make me feel very small and useless. I felt that way too. When I went to a local boarding school, I got nicknamed Mosquito because I was very tiny and again it reinforced how useless I was in my own eyes. I actually began to think that if my home people think that I am as good as chicken manure and these secondary school kids think I am a mosquito, surely there must be something wrong and with all this, my confidence vanished but my God had other ideas.

2. The Journey

It is when I look back, I truly do marvel at how magnificent God is. Our understanding is limited; I guess that's why King Solomon implores us not to lean on our own understanding (Proverbs 3:5–6). Trust the Potter and stay on the wheel as he moulds our life, our character and our responses to Him (Jeremiah 18). Through the good and the bad, the comfortable and uncomfortable, our Father is causing all things to work together for us.

Growing up, my aunt was an SEN (Special Educational Needs) teacher so my mother regularly used to tell my siblings and me of our aunt's encounters, at work. I don't know why but I adored hearing these stories, I was intrigued each and every time I listened to the stories. Little did I know that this was the seed which God was planting for both my future and my favour.

As much as I wanted to be a doctor (medical doctor), in my secondary years, reality began to kick in and priorities began to change. I had so many people I looked up to, especially my brothers. They were everything to me, and they still are, in many different ways. My brothers were intelligent; they truly did inspire me. Being the youngest, I had watched them succeed and achieve academically.

I had a little setback when I didn't achieve enough grades to go to university. At this point, I was interested in law but God had other ideas. I tried to re-sit my A-level exams twice as I was determined that I wanted to go to the only university in the country at the time. I didn't succeed. Looking back now I understand how Jonah fought against God's will until he ended up in a fish belly. Instead of going to university, I ended up at a teacher's training college against my will but that was the beginning of the journey to working with vulnerable young people.

I qualified as a history teacher in secondary education. Inspired by Mum's stories about my aunt's career in special needs, I developed a rare appetite for teaching children with special needs. I began to read about 'remedial classes' and how to help what were called 'slow learners' then.

Within a year of working in mainstream education I transferred to a SEN provision. It was a pioneering program to integrate deaf children into mainstream education. It was a daring move after I had visited education authorities without an appointment and requested that I be moved to somewhere that accommodated special needs children. I desired to work with disabled children (SEN) and up to now, I don't know why, but my desire has never diminished. I dreamt about it and I yearned to do it. This is what happens when God takes charge.

Although I was not qualified in SEN, I expressed an authentic interest in working in such settings. This desire was well communicated so I was transferred. This was one of the key moments in my life where God reminded me of David again. I was not qualified in man's eyes but God knew what I would do. He chose me and sent me away to do His work with deaf children.

This experience was absolutely remarkable. I worked with SEN children for a year or two and they taught me how to speak in Sign Language. I was seconded to go for further training in SEN by the regional office. Remarkably, I received a distinction in Sign language and teaching.

I was very active in organising sports for the disabled and my wife Molly was heavily involved too. These children became an extension of our family. We applied for funding and grants for computers so that the children and young people could receive an enriching experience.

Later, I knew it was time to further my education and professional development so I applied for further studies and The British Council offered me some funding to study in the United Kingdom. Although the requirements were a first-class degree which I didn't have, the Council felt that I needed to be sent abroad to gain more experience and to develop more. This is another of God's miracles, as out of the thirty-five people chosen in the country, I was the only person without a degree. All I had was my passion and burning desire to serve the vulnerable. Again, I was reminded of how God was watching over me. The funders had their own criteria but God had his, specifically for me. He chose me to go and study.

I completed a Bachelor of SEN, in England but unfortunately, there was no funding available to complete a Masters degree. My benevolent wife offered to work whilst I studied. We had £10,000 in savings. That's all we had to our name. The cost of the Masters programme was £9,000 but my wife convinced me that this was the right investment for our family. I remember cycling home one day, questioning what would come of this, with only £1000 left to our name. I then fell off my bike and broke my finger.

Fortunately, God provided for all our needs during my second year of studying. We never struggled with anything but we received an unexpected gift.

3. The Gift from God, the Hidden Blessing

When we were in Zimbabwe in 2004, we had our first child, a girl that we named Kupakwashe, meaning a gift from God. Kupakwashe was born prematurely at seven months so she was in an incubator for just four days until she passed away. The circumstances surrounding her death are still ambiguous. There was negligence and lack of explanation as to what really happened on the night she died. The senior nurse just told us that we were 'young enough to have many more anyway' so we were not supposed to worry. We were devastated and confused but didn't know what to do.

However, both Molly and I accepted that the devil has a vendetta against families. We knew the devil always attacks families and we took this as our attack and we were determined to win it by standing on God's word that He is with us and will not leave us alone. We were certain that God could and would heal us of the loss of our baby daughter.

In 2005, whilst I was still a student at the University of Birmingham and working part time as a carer, Molly discovered that she was pregnant. We were both elated and looked forward to the birth of our baby who was born, by caesarean, on 30 December 2005. Before knowing the sex of the child, both Molly and I had already decided that this child was going to be named Kupakwashe too, as he or she would also be a gift from God. Being filled with faith and irrespective of what we had both formerly endured, we were convinced this was our time to celebrate as we had already passed our test. We handled our daughter Kupakwashe's passing with dignity and we continued to trust in God.

When Kupakwashe (Kupa) was born, Molly and I were completely unprepared for what we were confronted with on that day. As soon as the midwives passed Kupa to me, I instinctively checked his palms for signs of Down 's syndrome. I don't know why I did this but I couldn't believe what I saw. I knew that people with Down 's syndrome have one long line running across their palm. I saw that exact line on the palm of my baby boy who tranquilly lay in my arms as I examined him. Molly was still in pain and dazed by the drugs from the operation but she said, 'He has funny eyes.' I knew this was another sign which I brushed off.

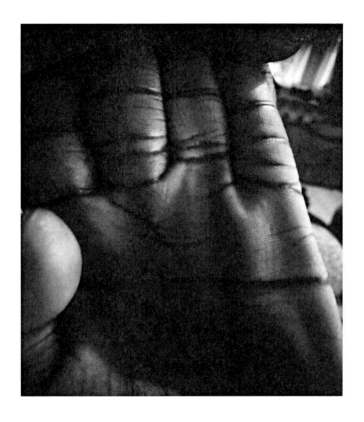

This is the palm that I first saw at the hospital when Kupa was born. The line that runs continuously across the palm is only unique to people with Down's Syndrome.

At this point, my mind was everywhere. I felt completely numb and confused. I was somewhat lost – lost in my thoughts, lost in my emotions and lost in my fears. Funnily enough, I had just completed a module at university on various disabilities, including Down's syndrome. I had also studied this disability in detail, back home in Zimbabwe. My mind raced from thinking about my son's education to his marriage, living independently and all of the other things I knew he would face in the future.

Not only that, but I also had the onus of telling my wife, who was still in pain from the caesarean, about our new reality. I decided not to disclose this to Molly just yet but alas, a young doctor (consultant) burst into our room. Looking hasty, she asked Molly and me what we knew about Down's syndrome but by this point, I could hardly hear her. Perhaps the consultant thought that I couldn't speak proper English but I desperately wanted her to shut up and go away. She said what she needed to say, which I can't recall, and then she left.

I reassured Molly. I told her that we would be OK and that we could still name our baby Kupakwashe because he was still a gift from God. It was getting late with the December darkness and cold, so I left the hospital and walked home. I actually forgot to catch the bus. Walking home felt better but that night, I cried myself to sleep.

I remember Nelson Mandela talking about 'feeling lonely in a crowd'. I think that's exactly how I felt. I felt very much on my own. I had so many questions to ask God. Likewise, there were many answers which I needed to hear. I couldn't understand the science of it all nor any of the explanations. How could this happen to me and my beloved wife when we had lost a baby just two years before? We weren't that old to have been at risk of having a baby with Down's syndrome and moreover, where was my God? None of it made any sense to me.

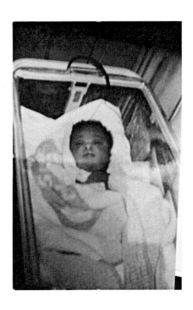

This is my first sight of Kupa in Hospital

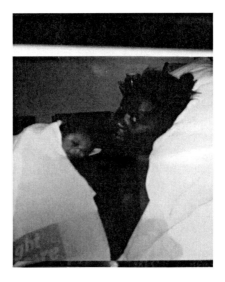

Molly bonding with Kupa

I battled that night with what the future for my family would look like. I was a little tormented as I remembered that in Zimbabwe, a work colleague had warned me that I was becoming obsessed with special needs and culturally there was a myth that it meant I was going to have a disabled child. I also remembered that growing up, I was always told that only men who were inadequate had disabled children. Whatever that meant, did that mean that I too was inadequate? Maybe I was only as good as my nickname, dokororo? Questions burdened me. They lay heavy on my heart. Had I done something wrong to God? Was this a punishment? Was this a curse of some sort? Would our next child be disabled too? What would our friends and family say? Later, I was reminded of the name Molly and I had given our son: Kupakwashe. This child was truly a gift from God.

Molly and I spent the next few days going through the difficulties of telling friends and family that '*we have been blessed with a baby boy but...*' It was horrible news! We were far away from home. We now lived in England and all of our family and most of our friends were in Zimbabwe. We had never felt that lonely before. The pain was made worse by the several appointments we had to attend to make sure that Kupa was 'OK'. I was pleased that Molly seemed to be coping well but I then realised that she hadn't considered Kupa's future.

When we got the news, because of my background knowledge, I had a full picture of what the battle ahead of us was so I was not oblivious to the challenges which we were to be confronted with. I knew it would hit Molly in milestones: like she would understand it when Kupa takes longer to learn to talk, walk and when he starts school. Considering her pain, I decided not to share my thoughts with my wife. I didn't tell her what I was thinking; she had enough pain to cope with.

I was offered time off from my studies to deal with my family's situation but I decided to carry on. My studies quickly became my therapy. I went into research mode and read anything and everything about Down's syndrome. It was emotional. I found both good and bad stories. Also, my mentor told me that people with Down's syndrome were loving and funny but also very stubborn. Some friends from university visited me and Molly, they helped us a lot. My course administrator and a few Zimbabwean friends were always there to help us too, with advice and encouragement. God never left us alone in our times of trouble.

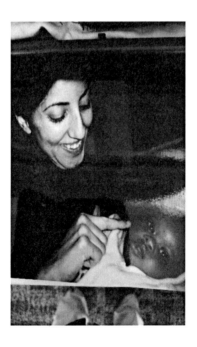

Marina has remained a close family friend since Kupa was born

God had not yet finished preparing me for the immense work ahead. Two years after Kupa was born, he was diagnosed with autism. I just laughed. I was now ready for anything. What else could come at us? As long as Kupa was alive and healthy, we knew we'd be fine. Molly and I started to learn to value the basic things, life and health. Kupa's paediatrician, who had diagnosed him, had been to Zimbabwe before so we bonded immediately. She was very good with our family. In a strange sort of way, I was excited about Kupa's new diagnosis and I happily shared the news with friends and relatives. I had renewed strength and happiness. Due to this, I decided that I was going to be a SEN specialist so that I could help others in my situation.

Despite the adversities, the vision was planted and the journey had started, unbeknownst to me. I was now armed with my son's SEN and a Master of Education in SEN degree.

Although I yearned for a PhD, God had other plans in my preparation for the big call.

I became very attached to my son

The business to bless others

In 2014, one of my friends from Zimbabwe was obedient to the call of God. He flew to England, from our home country, Zimbabwe, to kick start the work which God had been forming in me. In 2015, Interestingly, the last time I had seen him was 23 years prior to that, in 1991. He came to stay in the UK, with me for a few days. This was when I felt a further tugging so I knew that He had acted in purpose.

One evening, we were praying at some time around 11pm. He turned to me and asked if I had any prayer requests so I told him about my vision for the school. We prayed about it and soon after, he offered to put some money aside for us to start the school together. Amazingly, He was taught to have no fear and carpe diem (seize the day) because it was already blessed. That very night, together, we launched a company and registered everything until 5am the next morning. We practically did not sleep and I learned a valuable lesson that business is all about hard work. I was required to be at work for 7.30am. The reality of the magnitude of the vision caused sleeplessness and restlessness but 'everything is possible for one who believes' (Mark 9:23).

Although my friend left soon after setting up the company and was never involved in its development, I wasn't worried because God confirmed that he was a vision facilitator, not necessarily an active part of the vision. It is vital that we discern the capacity in which people are sent into our lives because if we mistake season people for reason people then we get discouraged, thinking that God has left us without, when really, we have been equipped with all that we need, within. Similarly, if we mistake people who are sent for a reason, with people who are sent for a season then the impartation will not occur as effectively. If we don't understand the purpose of individuals in our lives then we can miss what God is trying to transform us into, due to our emotions and thoughts concerning matters which God has already spoken over.

Not long after his departure, God introduced me to Anthony Copeland (Tony), an amazing Englishman who though he's not a Christian, upholds Christian values more than anyone I know. Initially, I was introduced to Tony as my landlord since I was supposed to rent the school building from him but upon further conversations, we discovered that we had too much in common and therefore there was no other way but to work together to push the Riverside vision.

I have always acknowledged that Tony was sent to me, by God, to provide all the resources to develop and stabilise Riverside. The combination of our skills is very unique. My expertise lies in the area of SEN and Tony is a very successful businessman. The amalgamation of our skills meant that the Riverside vision would have a fully rounded expertise in the area of working practically with the young people and in the area of business and financial literacy. Even now, years later, I facilitate the day to day running of Riverside whilst Tony facilitates the business and financial aspects of it.

For me, meeting and working with Tony was a miracle in and of itself. When we first met, Tony remembers assuring himself, "Yes, I can work with that small man." I was personally intrigued by Tony's interest in helping me and my vision. Above all, it was Tony's evident belief in his own values: honesty, integrity and respect which confirmed the hand of God in this. Everything was done on just a handshake. Tony and I have worked together for over five years and I have come to realise that Tony is literally 'a slave of his word'. He is integral through and through. Whatever he says he will do.

Over the five years of our business relationship and friendship, Tony has done everything he has promised to do and more. He has very strong morals, values and ethics. He likes people to be treated fairly and has respect for everyone, genuinely. Albeit these are values which I admittedly see my own Christian friends struggling with; even I struggle with these too. I was incredibly challenged by Tony's adherence to honesty, integrity and respect, so much so that I began to question my own faith. This reflection delineated to me how much I needed to develop, both as a Christian and as a person, generally.

Despite our diverse backgrounds, Tony and I are bound to each other by our values and passion. Our friendship and desire to develop each other is another fundamental to our success. Tony always affirms, "What matters is what happens between the two of us." The philanthropy of Tony was conveyed very early on. Tony promised to provide me with the finances to begin and develop Riverside.

Unquestionably, there was an evident risk that the school would be unsuccessful, resulting in Tony losing his money. During this conversation, Tony told me, "I want you to know that if I lose the money, it won't change my life and if you pay it back, it won't change my life either because I am financially secure already. I want this money to change your life and change the lives of the many people you will come into contact with, as a result of the work you do in the school." Hearing this, I could only hear God. I was assured that God was at work and God was indisputably in the midst.

Let's be real: how many people would give such a large amount of money to a stranger? I don't think Tony was always convinced. I remember meeting with him on several occasions to share the vision, he'd conclude: "I'm 70% convinced." Another time, it was, "I'm 80% convinced." Up until now, I am unsure what made Tony convinced 100% but what I do know is that when he gave me a yes, he had never shown anything but 100% belief and conviction in the Riverside vision.

At the same time Tony and I were actively opening Riverside, someone else was running a school on the same premises but had decided to close it due to the lack of students engaging. This revelation led to Tony questioning how they were going to find students when someone was closing due to disengagement. Another insane situation: a local person was closing a business of the same nature and I, a foreigner, was audacious enough to open the same business in the same premises, hoping to do better. Despite this seemingly impossible situation, the vision and our own convictions fuelled both Tony and I to continue on the journey to open Riverside. Tony invested and God did the rest. Deep down, I knew that 'I can do all this through him who gives me strength' (Philippians 4:13).

There is nowhere in this world that someone would give a stranger money and show such altruism by nonchalantly saying such powerful words. But God! During the aforementioned meeting, Tony went on to encourage me, saying that he desired to see what sort of a man I would be with and without money. "If you want to know a man, give him money and give him power." Money and power are such powerful commodities since they have the potency to reveal the best and worst parts of ourselves.

The words which Tony, as a man who once had no money and now has an incalculable amount, spoke to me that day, and it is these words that will keep me grounded. Tony always asked, "Without money, am I a better man than you?" That's the question we should always ask ourselves.

As mentioned earlier, Tony and I are two individuals from two extremely different backgrounds. Our values and work ethic are what has been focal to our success. Incredibly, within our business relationship, there is a partnership; neither makes decisions nor acts upon things without consulting the other. The most insane matter is that we have no written documents, binding any aspect of our business or partnership. In five years, we have been successful simply due to the respect which we have for each other and the integrity we possess within ourselves. We never signed any contracts; our solidarity was based on a verbal agreement. This can only be deemed as insane but when God is in the midst – greatness is destined. This whole experience makes no sense to man but it has been fruitful because whether knowingly or unknowingly, both Tony and I have simply obeyed God, despite how insane it looks to man. What's more, neither Tony nor I had the vision to chase money but were whole-heartedly appreciative when the money came anyway. We believe our business and partnership has been successful because our vision was always to help others. For this reason, contracts were never a priority.

I am a father of a child with SEN, I have a PhD in SEN and I now pride myself on the twenty plus years' experience I have, in the area of SEN. Tony, however, has a background in property development. He has no experience in SEN at all but amongst any other person I have ever met in my line of work, Tony has so much passion for SEN and helping vulnerable people, this was evident right from the start.

It truly has been unfathomable but as soon as I was transparent enough to tell Tony my story, Tony was intrigued and this intrigue was confirmed by his philanthropic actions. As one who initially shared the same passion as me for showing compassion and consideration to those with the greatest needs, I sometimes have to ask Tony to slow down.

Unashamedly, I now believe that Tony has more passion than me; I can only attribute this to God working in and through him.

To date, we have a school that accommodates over a hundred students across three sites employing over fifty staff. This means that meeting Tony has resulted in a positive impact of over one hundred and fifty families in the UK. I am aware this is not a lot but I always wonder if each of us aim to do good and have a positive effect on each other or on at least five families, this world will be a better place. I feel privileged that God has entrusted me with such influence and responsibility. The school will continue to grow and positively affect many lives in the future and this is the legacy I am leaving in this country.

Tony McGuire has been a part of Riverside Education since the beginning. He introduced me to key people who facilitated my first meeting with Tony Copeland. I call him a Riverside legend. He did all the hard work for free.

The discouragement in opening Riverside

God assures us that 'no weapon that is formed against thee shall prosper; and every tongue that shall rise against thee in judgment thou shalt condemn. This is the heritage of the servants of the LORD, and their righteousness is of me, saith the LORD' (Isiah 54 vs 17). My friend once preached that this does not mean that the weapons will not be formed, it means the weapons will be manufactured and thrown at you but they will not harm you. I experienced this as soon as Riverside was opened in September 2015. I suspected this would happen but not at the scale it happened. One of my friends called me a few weeks before we opened the school and she said, 'Abide you have to be in your school on the first day it opens. This is history and you will never have this moment again. Are you sure you don't want to witness it?' This was after I had told her that I would be staying in my old job for a few months since we only have one student starting with us and that once the student numbers began to rise, I would join the team. This was not true, I was afraid. Although the bible says, 'Fear not for I am with you' (Isiah 41 vs 10), I still had this fear that what if…

There was a time in which I felt like Moses. God sent Moses to Egypt to demand the release of the Israelites from Egyptian slavery. Remembering his inadequacies, Moses told God what he lacked (Exodus 3). Moses questioned how he could speak to Pharaoh when he was ill-equipped, for he had a speech problem. When I knew it was time to trust God and open Riverside, I too felt ill-equipped. Temporarily, I allowed people and the pain they birthed to sow seeds of doubt, making me feel as if I wasn't enough. Although I had Tony and resources provided, there was still a reminder of the absurdity of it all. At the back of my mind, I always asked myself if I was good enough for this.

As well as this, along the way, I had comments like, "People who look like you, don't do what you're doing." I was reminded of my colour, my limited abilities and my money, or lack thereof. The discouragement was great but the courage which God instilled in me was far greater. I have learnt that when God blesses you, your weaknesses are made strengths.

How I knew it was time to transition into and manifest the promise of God can be likened to the prompting which an eaglet encounters. Initially, mother eagles provide a nest which is densely padded with feathers. What most people don't know is that underneath the feathers is a base of branches, rocks and thorns. This is because when the eaglet has reached a stage of maturity, the mother eagle stirs the nest which involves the base of the nest being uprooted. The nest then becomes an unsuitable and uncomfortable environment for the eaglet. Eagles induce these conditions so that the eaglet is prompted to flee the nest and fly to unleash the power of their soar.

I reached a stage where I was passionate about my job but I was simultaneously frustrated. I had been in this job for almost 10 years. I had devoted so much to this organisation but I began to feel useless: my purpose was frustrated. I was uncomfortable but I also recognised that God was pushing and preparing to let His glory be revealed. I remember one day we woke to some heavy snow and I couldn't drive to work. Schools were advised to close for health and safety reasons. Knowing some of students would still come in anyway, I decided to walk the four miles to work in the snow. When I got there, it was just me and my boss. He was surprised to see me but that was how much I loved my job.

That job was another God-sent miracle to me. I got it when I applied to be a tutor but my application was declined. I called the manager to thank them for taking the time to consider my application. The manager and I got talking, he then offered me a position as an Education Mentor. I grew to love my role and was promoted a few times and ended up becoming the deputy head teacher responsible for the day to day running of the school. It was the best learning opportunity that equipped me to recognise that I possessed the capacity to facilitate a special needs school. At this stage, I had completed my PhD, I felt confident and had an inner desire to do something bigger and better for the children I was working with.

When God opens the doors for you

'If God is for us, who can be against us?' (Romans 8:31).

It is amazing what happens in life when God opens doors for you. I can personally testify that when God opens doors to bless you in life, no one can close them. He will soften the hearts of the hard hearted and he will send angels to protect you. He will give you the right words to say at the right time and he will manage your emotions. He did that for me.

When my friend flew from Zimbabwe, he had so much to teach me but I don't think he knows how much I learned from him. He was just talking generally but little did he know that he was opening up my brain to a lot of things. One evening after a prayer, he said to me, 'Tsano (brother), don't be afraid.' I don't know how he knew I was afraid but I held on to those words forever and up to now, when fear grips me, I hear his voice and I know it's God's voice.

After this encounter, everything seemed to fall into place. People volunteered to assist me, to take minutes during meetings, take care of paperwork and be instrumental in seeing the manifestation of my vision. Who could it be but God? Trustworthy friends who believed in my vision came and worked for free. This reminded me that God certainly provides the resources for those who adhere to His vision. I was never in need of anything. I was in very good health and in good spirits. I had my energy back and I was so focussed. I know a lot of people who take the gift of health for granted, I don't. Without good health, I would not have achieved His vison. I was working day and night whilst supporting Molly to look after the kids. God gave me that strength. Those who hope in the Lord will renew their strength. They will soar on wings like eagles; they will run and not grow weary; they will walk and not be faint. (Isaiah 40:31)

My vision was to use my education, experience and professionalism to help others. There was so much evidence of God's provision. I was granted Ofsted rating to open the school; God provided advisors to guide me every step of the way; I was spiritually empowered by pastors who prayed with and for me and Riverside. The pastors offered endless advice and even now, they still pray for us.

Everything came in at once: the help and the resources. This only consolidates that God opens doors which no man can shut. I had no money to pay anyone but so many people confessed that they had to be there for the day of the school's opening. I asked why and they said, "We will never have a chance of this first day again."

To God be the glory! I am still humbled by how much the school is changing lives. People are getting employed, disengaged children are getting educated and we have universities carrying out research projects in our school. That is God's doing. As an African boy growing up with no expectations but a derogatory nickname, in a foreign country, I always questioned whether it was possible. Nonetheless, along the way, I have learnt to quit the questions and make my faith fruitful.

It truly is extraordinary how one can come to a developed nation of this status and change people's lives in this way. Let's check God's track record: David was a shepherd boy who never thought of becoming a king one day but God had other plans. Moses had a speech problem yet was sent to speak to the Egyptians; incredibly, he negotiated the release of the Israelites from slavery. This is not just a cliché, neither is it just history. The God who did all of this many years ago is still in the miracle working business today. When God says yes, no one can say no for it is only He who can choose to make use of that and those whom we deem useless.

One of the greatest blessings is that the school passed Ofsted with 'Outstanding' in Management and Leadership in 2019. I was so overwhelmed that I cried for three consecutive days. How could I be 'Outstanding', with all that I have gone through in my life. All credit goes to God and the staff that are making it happen every day. Truly, the magnitude of the vision was unfathomable until all manifested. Even so, God provided people who ensured that I was equipped and facilitated in bringing glory to God's work and his people. People often prayed and dreamt which affirmed that my life was in the hands of God and that God's hands were undoubtedly on my life.

Below is one the quotes from an Ofsted inspector who visited our school. These are words that keep us going in tough times.

'Parents and carers speak highly of the school.' Typical comments included 'They will do anything for you' and 'They see their role as a vocation and not a job'.

Whatever is working against you, consider what is working for you. You may be focused on your disabilities but consider your abilities.

"Change your thoughts: change your life."

(Lao-Tzu)

It could only be God who instilled such zeal within me to ensure that the vision came into full fruition. Not only that, the fact that the vision has grown and has been sustained is evidence of God's plans and provision. God entrusted me with the vision, I heeded to the call and so God has been gracious in blessing my family and me with good health to remain faithful to His plans. People think I am gifted and intelligent but it's God's wisdom.

I am truly humbled by all that God has done and still does. Even through adversities, I see God. In my line of work, I am regularly abused, verbally and even physically. The abuse inspires me to persevere and reveal God. When a member of staff asked me how I remain so calm in such volatile situations, I replied: "He who is in me is greater than he who is in them." This perspective echoes and testifies in every area of my life. I've been through so much and God has given me so much not to trust and believe in Him.

The weapons will continue to be fired

My business partner, Tony has taught me that Honesty, Integrity and Respect are values that if one adopts, they will always win. I have always seen these values as rooted in my Christian beliefs. I don't believe that if someone does evil to me, I have to be evil to them too. I believe that my values will fight for me. I don't have to go around telling people what I am like but deeds, my work and passion will speak for itself. Just like most of us, I am still a work in progress as the weapons continue to be fired against what we do in our work.

Once in a while we still receive anonymous calls about how bad we are doing. We also have people we do not know and have never met still reporting us to the authorities alleging that we have done things that we have not done. Our values always fight for us and I personally believe this is good for the children we work with because we end up providing the best education for them as we are constantly monitored. Our standards have risen as a result of these malicious false reports. A good result for the students, that's how God works sometimes.

Wanting to help everyone where I can, I employed people who later proved to be against both my values and the school's ethos. They would challenge everything I did or say as if that was the only thing they were employed to do. This was disheartening but all of my previous encounters equipped me to deal with God's counsel. I learned 'to be still'. Exodus 14:14 The LORD will fight for you; you need only to be still

(Exodus 14 vs 14). Along the way, I have lost friends and family who struggled to understand my work. My passion has been misconstrued as an unhealthy obsession but this wasn't just a job or a business, this was what God created me for. This is obedience which is better than sacrifice. I have always found solace in remembering that Jesus also had the same issue. Like Jesus, I am about his Father's business (Luke 2:49). Sometimes the 'Father's business' requires us to leave everything and follow Him, He will take care of everything. He has taken care of my family and my health as well as all my needs.

Ultimately, the battles I've had have made me so much more appreciative of every blessing which God has gifted me with. Having God in you makes you see people differently. Truly it is a case of 'Father, forgive them for they know not what they are doing' (Luke 23:34). God allows such challenges to keep us humble enough to desire and utilise His power, presence and love. When we find the strength to call out to God, during our most vulnerable times, He definitely strengthens us and provides the evidence to our faith. When we check the records in our own life and see how God made a way, time after time – we truly have no reason to fear when facing trials. God truly provides a 'ram in the bush': He provides a way through and out.

Managing failure

I recently read Michelle Obama's book titled 'Becoming Michelle Obama'. I was inspired and tutored at the same time. She grew up in poverty but worked hard and ended up sitting on the same table with some of the most influential people in the world. She achieved a lot but there were certain times that she also had setbacks and losses. I liked how she dealt with her losses and failures. However, what struck me most was that when she sat on the same table as the people, she thought were high and mighty, she found out that they were as ordinary as her and she was even far better than some of them. God has made us all unique in our own ways and we can be influential in different ways, big and small but still making a positive impact on people's lives. We can fail too but it doesn't mean we have to give up. There is a big difference between the two.

During the early days of opening Riverside, we failed an Ofsted inspection. At this time, the school was still growing in numbers. It was as if God was asking me whose report was, I going to believe. Surely, it knocked my confidence but just like Abraham, I had to remind myself of God's promises.

God spoke to Abraham and told him that He was going to bless Sarah, his wife's womb (Genesis 17:16). Abraham was astonished because both he and his wife were already old, in age. The promise tarried but eventually, when Abraham was one hundred years old, his wife gave birth to their son Isaac.

As with Abraham, many naysayers were around. People wondered, "Are you sure God told you this?" I was sure. I also had so many staff members who had given up everything because they believed in the vision. We worked hard: tirelessly. We knew Ofsted would come back and when they did, we needed their report to align with God's. The team continued to shine their brightest and make transformations so that next time, they would get the grading which they knew they were deserving of. We stayed true to our values, prayed and trusted God. I remember one member of staff asking if I should appeal the Ofsted rating and I said no, Ofsted will come back within two years and if we are good or better, we will prove ourselves and indeed with God's help we proved ourselves. I called upon trusted friends to pray with me and as usual, my wife was by my side doing what she does best – praying. During the two years of working hard and prayer, my friends saw visions of Riverside expanding and growing in numbers and indeed in two years we rose from forty students to over one hundred.

It is common knowledge that Thomas Edison, the first commercially viable light bulb inventor, *failed* 999 times but he kept trying. With that being said, we are reminded that what we deem failure as real practise: we only fail if we give up trying. Despite the daunting Ofsted report, we continued to develop ourselves and our practice. We took a lot of risks that included applying for material change twice which if we had failed, we could have been in a worse position. We ignored the negative reports and focussed on providing the best education for our students. All outstanding people take risks, they have enemies but they are resilient and tenacious enough to overcome challenges. At Riverside Education, we are working hard to be on the same table as the best of the best. As I said before, we are a work in progress.

Throughout this whole process, I have learnt lessons which keep me humble, knowing that God is mindful of me. Challenges cannot confine me because I have learnt: the bigger the challenge, the bigger the blessing. Challenges simply remind me that it's not by my own might, nor is it by my own power: it is only by the spirit of the Lord that I am able to achieve (Zechariah 4:6). If you want to grow, have the ability to learn and the willingness to change.

The devil loves failure. He will do anything to put you down. He is a thief. He will steal your confidence and he will steal your passion too. He stole everything from Job but because he believed in God, everything was restored. Just a tip: when the devil reminds you of your past, remind him of your future for God still has good plans for you!

I have been blessed with the grace to communicate and build relationships with people from an eclectic of backgrounds. I know that God desires for me to keep the same friends whilst still making myself available and of service to the vulnerable young people and their families. Humbled by this calling, I still light up at the sight of my students and their parents.

The lessons learnt

The journey of my life has been a revelation to myself. I have learnt a lot about myself. I am now able to reflect on all that I have done well and most importantly all that I have not done so well. I look back to the past and think about what I could have changed – nothing, but I could have done better in a lot of areas, though I would not change anything.

Below are some of the things I have learned in my short journey of life:

Whatever you do, do it for the glory of God. Money will come as a consequence. Chase God's vision and He will provide the resources. Most importantly, He will provide fulfilment and fortitude. The other things we chase may very well produce fruit, but fulfilment may be absent. 'Seek the Kingdom of God above all else, and He will give you everything you need' (Luke 12 vs 31). Have faith that if you pursue Him, He will take care of everything.

I have learned not to despise myself because of my mistakes. My weaknesses and mistakes do not disqualify me from anything because in actuality, God is a God of the turnaround: He can make you wiser as a result of your mistakes. It took me four attempts to set up a school; I succeeded on the fifth attempt but I know that God knew that I wasn't ready up until that point.

We serve a God who delights in transforming our weaknesses into strengths. English isn't my first language so I have to speak slowly and carefully; most of my students think that my speech delineates how calm and measured I am. For the most part I am calm and measured but the main reason behind my slow and meticulous speech is because English is not my native tongue. Therefore, my vocabulary is limited; hence I have to carefully choose the right words from the limited vocabulary bank that I have. My students have taught me so much. They are funny, argumentative and they seek an explanation to everything. I have learned to pick my battles carefully with them. My calmness and careful choice of words always wins when my students are hyper, upset and argumentative.

I have learned not to dwell on the past. God renews me every day. I am a new creation as a result of God's grace. When you concentrate on the past, it gives you limited vision or for the most part, a distorted vision for what God has for your future. It's like driving a car whilst looking in the rear-view mirror all the time. The likelihood of having an accident is highly probable; therefore, you will struggle to, or even fail to, reach your destination. Focus on the future and 'run towards the mark'. When writing to the Philippians, Paul admitted,

"I press towards the mark for the prize of the higher calling in God in Christ Jesus" (Philippians 3:14).

Even prior to this (Philippians 3:13), Paul encourages us to forget the things which are behind us so that we can press forward. We cannot do both: if we are focused on our past, how can we see our future? Accept the past and let that propel you deeper into your potential to manifest a fruitful future.

When writing to the Colossians, Paul encouraged that their service should be genuine, as their service was onto God, not man (Colossians 3:23–24). We can take this same encouragement. Whatever we do, know that it is for the Lord so work at it with all of your heart. Also, our reward may not be seen or revealed here on earth, or in our lifetime but the Lord is our reward and our rewarder. Do not be dismayed. Do not be discouraged. Let your desire drive you; know that it is God whom we are serving.

More recently, I am influenced and inspired by Captain Tom Moore who at the age of 99 raised millions of pounds for the NHS. Before his 100th birthday, the Second World War veteran walked 100 laps of his back garden. Others were moved by his philanthropy so they gave generously, resulting in Captain Tom Moore raising over £9m for the NHS during the 2020 Covid 19 pandemic. Captain Tom's story conveys that it's not too late. Start now!

On a practical note, surround yourself with positive people so that negativity cannot consume you. God is always positive concerning you and your future. God is always willing us to do better and be better. God's plans and thoughts towards us are good and not evil. He plans to give us hope and an expected end and his plans are of hope and an expected end (Jeremiah 29:11). Why then should we absorb that which is a dichotomy to the Father's plans for our lives?

Be attentive to the voice of God. As much as you can try, some people cannot be helped but if it is God's will for you to assist them, then be obedient to that. Be careful though, people who do not bear fruit of change can serve as a distraction.

Do not be ignorant: the devil will intensify his work as you near your goals. My journey to opening Riverside had almost the same difficulties and excitement as the Israelites in the wilderness. At one point I was threatened with court action if I proceeded to open Riverside. Nevertheless, I also encountered the miracle of people I had never met come to assist me.

Knowing who you are is very important. I call it 'quiet confidence'. People will look at you and judge you and then label you. This label then deems the place we are given in society but God's label is the only label which truthfully matters. It is essential that we discern and listen to God's voice: learn to listen to God's voice, identify His voice and follow it up.

At Riverside, every day is a lesson and a blessing filled with new experiences and new knowledge. I meet different kinds of people, some challenging and others helpful but all useful. I am learning that in order to grow, one must go into new territory. Again, the discomfort I spoke of earlier must be experienced and sometimes this discomfort is due to unfamiliarity. Ways to develop Riverside and make it a better place to work is always at the forefront of my mind. Riverside prides itself on reflective practice; we look through a critical lens to uphold the best practice, through the complicated academic research process called Participatory Action Research (PAR).

I become very academic when I speak about PAR. I sat for many hours talking about PAR with my PhD supervisor who is still my mentor today. As much as it was an academic conversation, I always brought it back to my religion, God wants us to reflect on our deeds all the time and it has been lesson for life plucked from an academic conversation. Always look for what God is trying to tell you through different people. Moses spoke to God through a burning bush. Find your own 'burning bushes' and you will find God.

Both myself and my senior team are currently learning that to achieve what you have not yet achieved; you must attempt what you have not yet attempted. All this is through our past experiences, both the good and bad. At Riverside, we are always eager to explore and attempt new things to push past boundaries. Though we are not always successful, we fathom that we will never be successful until we have the courage to try.

The Bible talks a lot about fear because it is an emotion which many of us experience several times a day which would equate to an incalculable amount during our lifetime. One of the most excellent revelations about fear is found in Isaiah 41:10–13.

"Fear not for I am with you."

It's not complicated: it really is as simple as that.

Dealing with fear

"Don't be afraid of them. Remember the Lord, who is great and awesome." (Nehemiah 4:14).

I briefly spoke about fear previously but I want to expand on it some more because in my experience, fear is the biggest weapon the devil uses to prevent us from doing God's work. Fear questions your ability and it makes you think about things going wrong only. Fear has no positives in it. Even as I write this book, fear is telling me that no one will read it and its going to be a complete failure. That's fear for you.

There are so many things that we encounter that we fear. Whilst growing up, I was fearful of darkness and thunder. Due to my fear of thunder, I slept in my parents' room until I was twelve years old. When Kupa was born, I was gripped by a different kind of fear. My fear wasn't so much attributed to disproportionate or illogical thinking, like it was when I was younger, but this fear was induced by the reality that someone I loved would be subject to being treated inhumanely due to others' ignorance.

As alluded to in previous chapters, during this time, I didn't realise that God was with me, even during a time in which I felt extremely lonely. Even during the tumultuous challenge, when others wanted Riverside to fail, I was afraid then also. I feared for myself and my family too. I feared I would lose my job. I feared that I would let down those who so readily helped me. For those who I had employed, I feared that I would have to let them go. How then would they be able to provide for their families? The fear was relentless and spiralling out of control. But God!

An unknown writer once said that 99% of the things we fear never happen. Another person added that when we fear, we put ourselves through the trauma twice, unnecessarily: firstly, we conjure up the worst scenario(s) and experience all of the negative emotions associated with it; secondly, when we actually go through the situation, we experience the trauma again – with all real and imaginary anxieties attached. Let's not talk about how we allow memories of it to hold us hostage, again and again and again. Looking back, in retrospect, I realise that I never did actually encounter what I had feared.

Providing that we continue to put everything in God's hands, we will always see God's hands on everything. As long as you give God the credit for your success, He will continue to use you and bless you. When opening Riverside, I told God that it was His place. My prayer was, "God, please make this place your dwelling." Oftentimes, I hear others conclude that Riverside has a *different feel*. I can do nothing but praise God because He truly has made Riverside His dwelling place – others feel it too. They are noticing is confirmation that God is still moving in the school.

4. The Challenges in the Blessing

Kupa's journey from childhood to adolescence has been challenging: hormones do not discriminate. Kupa is now becoming a man but he does not know how to handle himself and cope with the changes going on in his body. When Kupa is angry, he can hit, bite and scratch. It's something which the family can manage at the moment though we wonder how manageable these behaviours will be, as we grow older and weaker. Also, Kupa's sleeping patterns have changed, as well as his eating habits. Sometimes he gets moody or even excited for no apparent reason. All these are issues which Molly and I are navigating through.

Kupa can get obsessed with certain things: his current obsession is with plastic bags from ASDA. He loves them and as soon as he gets one, he won't let it go until he goes to bed. He will tear it into very small pieces; he enjoys doing this for his own sensory satisfaction. My family and I regularly reminisce on an incident in which we hid all of the plastic bags in the house just to get some respite from Kupa causing a mess in the house. Like I said, we hid all of the bags, or so we thought. Kupa knew that there were some plastic bags in the deep freezer so he woke up around 2am and took a plastic bag from the freezer that was full of some tomatoes from our family's allotment. He decided to give me and Molly back our tomatoes by throwing them on our bed.

We woke up in the middle of the night to be greeted by very cold 'objects' on our bed. We wondered what was going on – only to discover that our bed was full of thawing tomatoes. When we went to check on Kupa, he was busy in his bedroom playing with the plastic bag which once held the tomatoes.

Kupa would rather spend the whole day shredding plastic

Though Kupa will soon be sixteen years old, he is still in nappies. It is a massive challenge; sometimes I ask myself if I could have done better to toilet-train him. As a first child and with no experience of looking after any other child, I believe it's an area which I could have learned more and done better in. I say this because I have seen other children, like Kupa, who are toilet-trained.

In 2014, the family and I visited Zimbabwe. Kupa surprised everyone by requesting to go to the toilet and he did so, for the duration of time that we were there (two weeks). Despite our desperate efforts, when we returned to the UK, Kupa returned to his previous routine. With Kupa's unique behaviour and toilet needs, it is difficult to visit other families too. There are only a few families that Molly and I feel are comfortable having Kupa in their house so this adds to the isolation issues that families like mine are subject to.

I always like to think that if God allows us to go through some difficult times and grief, there is a reason and purpose for it. Living with Kupa is an everyday challenge and I am always thinking about what God wants me to see or learn from the challenges I face. When Jacob wrestled against God, (Genesis 32:22–32) he dislocated his hip in the process. Jacob received his blessing but walked with a limp for the rest of his life. That limp was purposed to remind him of who God is. I always see Kupa as my limp, to remind me of who God is. I am honoured that my son and I are only going to be separated by death. It is a blessing – not a burden – that Kupa will be in my care forever.

Below is a picture of Kupa sitting on the pavement during a walk around the city and County of Cardiff, in Wales. Kupa does what he likes when he likes to do it. He has very little understanding of what's going on around him; he will sit anywhere whenever he feels like sitting. This can be problematic if you are in the middle of the city centre like in this case or if you are in a hurry. However, it's always Kupa's time, most of the times we see the funny side to it. In the past, I used to pick him up and proceed but now I can't, since he' is too big and too heavy for me to even attempt to pick him up, never mind carry him.

We were walking towards a beach in Cardiff, Kupa saw a pavement he liked and decided to sit there. This happens many times on our walks.

These days, my only option is to try and negotiate with him. I have to try my utmost best to persuade him until he agrees to move on or on many occasions, we have had to abort the activity altogether. I was very frustrated when my application for a Blue Badge was turned down mainly because I had stated that Kupa can walk. It is an absolute blessing that Kupa can walk but what most people don't realise is the excess time needed to carry out simple activities because as aforementioned, Kupa does things in his own time.

Unfortunately, I have made two attempts to appeal for a Blue Badge, with no success.

We rarely travel by plane these days. If we are flying, we have to fly on separate occasions. Someone has to stay with Kupa, at home. Our flights to go back to Zimbabwe have always been a challenge, with Kupa, as they take an average of twenty hours. There is currently no direct flight to Zimbabwe from the UK and the cheapest option is to go via Dubai, Zambia then Zimbabwe. Kupa will not sleep on the plane. He will get agitated due to the constant changes and being confined to small space frustrates him all the more.

Kupa had once thrown food at the other passengers on a plane to Egypt. We were asked to clean up, by the cabin crew so since then, we have stopped flying with Kupa. Although I refused to clean up, it was a very embarrassing episode where I felt like I needed to explain to the whole plane that my son was autistic and was not intentionally delineating disruptive behaviours. The stares revealed all of the assumptions and disapproval of the other passengers. This is something which Molly and I are regularly subject to.

Another year, we were travelling to London on a train, Kupa was still very young, aged three or maybe even four. He stood up, went to a bearded Asian man who was fast asleep and pulled his beard. The man woke up in shock but was very understanding. Again, I had to apologise profusely. Although it was hilarious at the end, it was one of the many enigmatic episodes we face time and time again. There are so many other incidents in which Kupa has grabbed strangers inappropriately and we had to go and apologise. Luckily, it is very rare that the people get annoyed once they understand the situation.

I must say, I have met a lot of people who have been empathetic and sympathetic. I remember one evening, Kupa and I were at the Birmingham Airport waiting for Molly. It was a nightmare because Kupa doesn't like waiting. Again, unless it is us waiting for him but Kupa does not like waiting for on others. I was having difficulties controlling him. He was running around, touching people inappropriately and making 'weird' noises. One gentleman came up to me just to say, "I admire what you are doing, I know how difficult it is," and he walked away. It was strange but I felt it was God willing me on, telling me not to give up.

Kupa likes his food a lot. He eats very well to the amazement of people who visit our house. Kupa needs no assistance with feeding. However, when he starts eating, he doesn't know when to stop. We have to lock away all of the food all of the time. Kupa eats anything edible he finds around the house; this includes searching the bins which we have to keep locked away. I worry a lot about his weight and diet. So far, it's all good but he needs constant weight monitoring and a strict diet because he doesn't do much exercise. Nonetheless, he is always moving around the house which is helpful as it is a form of exercise.

If we want to go out and eat at a restaurant as a family, it has to be well planned in advance but it doesn't always go to plan. Molly and Kudzy (Kupa's brother) will have to go in first and order the food. They will then have to text or call me on my mobile when the food is on the table because Kupa has no capacity to wait. All he wants, is to eat and go back in the car. This means I have to eat as fast as him because if he finishes before me, I will have to leave my food and follow him to the car. He will either choose to go to the car or go on other people's tables and grab their food. On many occasions, Kupa has gotten upset and thrown the food across the room, messing up the floor and other people's food in the process.

In a restaurant with Kupa

My biggest challenge is due to the communication challenges that Kupa has. I will never be able to tell if he has a headache or any other invisible worries. He will never be able to tell him if he is worried about anything or ask me any questions that every son wants to ask his father. If there are no signs of illness, I just have to assume that Kupa is OK, which is not the most reliable indicator. His only indicators are smiles or cries. Although he makes various sounds to indicate his desires, they are not enough for me to understand his needs.

As a family, we have struggled with some ordinary things that 'a *normal* family' wouldn't think of as a struggle. Kupa's hygiene has been a massive challenge. He only likes brushing his teeth when he is in the bath – yes, physically in the bath. He prefers to have a bath instead of shower which is very helpful but can be expensive with water bills. Every time he gets in the bathtub, which is every morning, he brushes his teeth and the same before he goes to bed. He hasn't yet understood that he can brush his teeth without being in the bath.

A visit to the dentist is another challenge. It's something I personally dread because I cannot do anything to help. It takes a very understanding dentist to allow me to handle Kupa in a certain way for him or her to see his teeth. Most dentists I have met think that they can just tell Kupa to open his mouth and he will comply. When Kupa refuses, they don't understand why and it takes me to physically open his mouth which is a struggle. The dentists will have very few seconds to look into Kupa's mouth whilst I restrain him and it is not a nice thing for Kupa or me.

Encounters like this cause him immense stress but the only other option is to put him to sleep. I worry a lot about his dental health. It's OK for now but the future is uncertain. We just have to give him the best possible diet to maintain good and healthy teeth.

On one visit to the Children's Hospital in Birmingham Kupa just sat on the floor in the hospital's corridors and I had four generous professionals trying to help to get to his appointment. Usually, he refuses to wait at the reception and on many occasions, most medical professionals agree that we stay with Kupa in the car until they are ready for us so that we can just walk straight to his doctor.

Two years ago, Kupa's passport expired. I needed to apply for a new one. We went to the local pharmacy to have his passport photos taken. It was one of the biggest challenges I had not foreseen. He had to keep his head straight, close his mouth and stay still, all at the same. Kupa could not do this. It was impossible. We didn't know how to explain this to him. The photographer tried forty-seven times but they were all not good enough until I took it upon myself to choose the best one. I then had to write an accompanying letter to the passport office. Luckily it was accepted though I am dreading the next time we will have to do this again.

I cut Kupa's hair myself. He has only been to the barber's once and it didn't work. He didn't like the chair, the noise and everything about the place. I have never bothered to try again, knowing how much he hates change. Cutting his hair at home is very easy and he seems to enjoy it. Unfortunately, he has grown into a teenager and it has come with new challenges. There are other hairs I have to cut and Kupa doesn't like it. So far it has been very challenging.

Kupa likes everything to stay as it is in the house. We always find it hard to change furniture or even his bedding. When we moved house in 2019, after eleven years of living at the same address, it was a big challenge. We had to set up his bedroom in the very same way as it was in the old house and we added his sensory equipment. It was very successful but Molly had to take him back to the old house to show him that there was nothing there. Thankfully, Kupa quickly adapted as we maintained the same furniture for a while.

He still has his chair and bed from the old house. He has the same colour bedding. He drinks from the same cup all the time. He is very good at noticing if anything has been moved around the house. He will quickly put it back. Sofas, vases, chairs and fridges are kept in the same place all the time or there is no peace in the house. Kupa will notice if cupboards and drawers are not properly closed. He will not sit down until everything is in its place.

We like to keep the house very clean but as mentioned earlier, Kupa has a very interesting hobby of shredding plastic bags or paper – anything that he can lay his hands on. Anything plastic is shredded to the smallest imaginable pieces; this includes shopping bags and tissues. It is very difficult to predict what kind of plastic he is going to be interested in. Sometimes we buy fruit and put away plastic bowls but the next thing is that they are all shredded on the floor. At times, Kupa likes to keep all the shredded paper behind the radiators. We have to regularly check for this as this is a potential fire hazard.

What is most challenging about all of this is the level of alertness we all have to have around the house or anywhere we are with Kupa. There is no rest and we end up blaming each other on who was supposed to be watching Kupa. It's a constant battle and when you feel like you can't even relax, not even for a minute, in your own house, it becomes more like self-imprisonment. It is just exhausting: you end up not being as efficient as you would like to be – at home and at work.

5. God's Revelation and His Blessing

For every first-time parent, having a child is not an easy task. Though there are countless books which vow to prepare first-time parents, I am yet to come across one that prepares a first-time parent to have a disabled child. Even so, there is no manual for parenting, perhaps because parenting is meant to be guided by our natural instinct. Every child, disabled or not, is unique in their own way and parents have to make adjustments to make things work. Having watched a television programme called Britain's Best Parent, I noted that at the end of each series, the conclusion is always that every parent tries their best and there are many ways of parenting that can be deemed 'good'.

Like every other person, Kupa has his own personality and he makes sure he has a voice in the house which is heard. Having a person of Kupa's character, disability and personality has taught my family a lot of things. Kupa has taught us all to be patient and to try to understand other people from their own point of view. Kupa's life provides ours with perspective. As adults, Molly and I now try to get into his head so that we can think, feel and understand, like Kupa. Our family has learned to ask ourselves: *if we were Kupa, how would we feel about this?*

It could be something as trivial as food, or a holiday experience, a TV programme or every other possible situation. Our family has become very open-minded and acceptant, not only of Kupa's needs but other people's diverse needs too and it has made us better people because of this. Every day is a new day to learn, to convey growth and to love one another.

Many of my prayers have been centred on Kupa improving on many things such as his speech and his awareness of himself and others. Admittedly, I get worried about his future and many other things though I remain grateful because when I contemplate on such situations, God reveals Himself and provides me with some fascinating answers, reminders and revelations, as it were.

God continues to remind me that Kupa is both healthy and happy. He is not in any pain and he has an easy routine that makes life pleasant and seamless for him. I recognise my blessing, our family's blessing. Some parents spend most of their time in hospital with their children but my family does not. Kupa is physically very strong and we are actually quite fortunate that he doesn't know this. If Kupa knew how much strength he possesses, that could be a potentially volatile situation for others. Knowledge of his physical strength could enable Kupa to manipulate people and situations to get what he wants; thankfully, most of the times, he just accepts when the family says no to something.

In addition to all of this, Kupa is funny and creative. He is always making happy noises and watching music on TV. He has his own way of entertaining himself with the toys that he makes himself. One of his most admirable characteristics is that he takes joy in making others laugh. He is tidy, when he doesn't have a plastic bag or paper, and he cleans up after mealtimes, ensuring everything is in its place. Molly and I always joke that if he were to get a job, he would be very good at clearing tables in a restaurant.

As mentioned earlier, Kupa thrives off routine. He never misses school. He likes attending school and always waits for his bus to arrive. After school, he loves taking very long baths and playing in the water. His love for bathing helps Molly and me with Kupa's hygiene; he is willing to take as many baths as possible in each day.

The birth and development of Kupa has been a revelation on many levels. His birth changed my perspective on my expectations as a parent and his development is teaching me something new every day. Above all this, the experience of looking after Kupa has helped me to empathise with the parents I work with. I feel their emotions every time I speak to them and I can feel their trust in me that I will do the best for their children. With God's help, I am confident of this.

Working with other professionals to support Kupa

We have had a lot professionals coming to our house and we have had good and bad experiences of working with professionals. In my professional capacity I am also privileged work with over one hundred parents in and around Birmingham. It is part of my job that I am really proud of. I get to hear some very inspiring stories and I get to share my story too. Part of this job allows me to empathise with parents as we experience almost the same joys and sorrows in our journeys.

In the fifteen years we have had Kupa, he has managed to escape from the house three times. The first time, we had a delivery and the delivery man forgot to close the door and Kupa escaped without anyone noticing. The second time, we had builders in the house and they forgot to close the gate on the back garden and Kupa escaped again. On the third occasion, I decided to listen to some music with Kupa in the car parked in our drive. This is something that Kupa likes to do. I decided to go back in the house to collect something and Kupa escaped. On all occasions Kupa was brought back by the police after they were alerted by members of the public. On all occasions we were ashamed and felt inadequate. I remember one of our neighbours coming to give me a lecture on how to look after Kupa. He even went on to remind me that 'this was the UK, not an African village'. I felt that his comments were inappropriate and I regrettably told him where to go and we never spoke again until we moved. On all occasions that we had the police in our house, they were very polite and understanding of our situation. We were very grateful of their help and up to now I have so much respect for the police in this country. I work with them in my profession as well and I find them to be very helpful and professional.

Kupa's teachers have been amazing to work with. I attend some of the Education and Health Care Plan (EHCP) meetings and parent's evenings. In 2019 Kupa received a few awards one of which was for maintaining a hundred percent attendance. I was very proud of him. He likes school a lot which means that his teachers look after him well. We are always in constant communication with them and they give us very encouraging feedback. He used to have an amazing pastoral manager by the name Jackie. It was very easy to see that she had a calling to work with SEN children and their parents. She was one of those professionals that you just want to talk to even though you have nothing to say.

It hasn't been smooth sailing with the social services. I do not know why, but we always had black social workers being sent to our house and I was shocked by some of the things they said to us. On one occasion one social worker came to tell us to stop 'moaning' about Kupa because he was a child and did not 'ask to be born'. She went on to make comments such as we shouldn't be thinking about Kupa going into care because it was not a black a culture. One of the social workers told my wife how lucky she was to have a husband otherwise she would be on her own with Kupa. My wife was very upset with both social workers and we ended up requesting that they be changed. It has not been all bad though, we had one very good lady who sat, listened and understood our plight. She drew up a package to support both us and Kupa which included some respite care. This is something we were denied by the so called 'black social workers' who were assumed to be more understanding to our culture. All we wanted was someone to listen to our issues and find help if it was possible.

Kupa now goes for respite care after every three to four weeks and that is very helpful for our mental well-being. It also affords us an opportunity to be parents to his brother Kudzy who I will speak about later. Though we do not intend to put Kupa in full time care, he enjoys going to his respite. The staff do their best and are very welcoming. We currently have a family support worker who looks after Kupa and all of us as a family and its very helpful.

As a fellow professional myself and experiencing what some parents experience, I encourage other professionals to be more sensitive and understanding. Parents like me go through a cocktail of emotions and we need a bit of looking after. I am grateful that I have my God with me who promised that He will never leave me nor forsake me (Deuteronomy 31:6).

Finding your purpose

I hold a strong belief that God puts each and every one of us here on earth for a purpose. I enjoy watching documentaries in the media and across the world, particularly those about Africa and its richness. Having watched a lot of British people who have gone over to Africa to save various animals, I recognise that without directly quoting the Bible, many speak about their cause and mission with so much passion, and they call it a 'calling'. One person actually admitted that they do not understand their own fascination with Africa; she didn't understand why she was drawn to the motherland so much. Yet, I see God's calling in these people who travel to help; I recognise their purpose on this earth.

Up until I began to work with young people with SEN and their families, I struggled to understand my own calling and purpose. The joy and fulfilment which I get from this is second to none. The impact and influence, which I see, kindness and compassion can have, empowers me to continue to give, even when I see no physical, instant or personal rewards. As most people go through these processes surrounding their purpose, it is important that we acknowledge the highs and lows of this journey.

The scriptures will forever be my manual for encouragement, empowerment and evolution. During King David's time of distress, he encouraged us to:

'Call upon the Lord when in distress, He will not disappoint you.'

(Psalm 118.)

God has shown me that I have to acknowledge Him in every season. Yes, he already knows how we feel but just as in the physical; our social relationships thrive off communication. God wants us to communicate with him: tell him of our greatest joys and most dismal lows. Even in our times of distress, God desires to comfort us and provide us with a way through. I too have struggled immensely with certain people and certain situations; I have spent sleepless nights thinking about how I could resolve problems, only for the problem to solve itself. I have learnt to ask God to go before me, be around me and within me always, and God has never failed.

6. The Future

You will never walk alone

Although I am a devoted Arsenal fan, the headline always associated with Liverpool Football Club is one which has spoken volumes, throughout my life. I admire the Liverpool team a lot, this began in my childhood days, during the era of Ian Rush and Bruce Grobbelaar. Liverpool Football Club and its supporters have a history of both pain and joy but they always vowed that they are never alone.

It is unrecognisable where the team draw their strength from but their positivity and productivity remain a huge inspiration to me. Could it be that they are talking to God without knowing it? With God on my side, I too am reminded that I am not alone. As the scriptures say,

'God never leaves us nor does he forsake us.'

(Hebrews 13:5)

The Liverpool players never feel like they are on their own because they know that they have an army of fans and through that support, they can achieve anything. Such support has enabled the club to pull up some incredible, unanticipated victories. Liverpool Football Club is known for winning almost impossible matches, Milan in 2005 and Enfield in 2020 are some the matches that got the attention of even those who do not watch football. Despite all of the odds, they have won in the most unlikely of circumstances. Anything is possible to Liverpool Football Club, with their fans behind them. Likewise, with God on my side, I too feel the same way: I can do anything. Be encouraged, the same is applicable to you: with God on your side, you can do anything.

"After losing to Manchester City by a single point last year, we found fuel in our loss." These were the words spoken by one of Liverpool's players, James Milner, when Liverpool won the 2019/2020 premier league after thirty years of trying. They actually found inspiration in their loss. This response was incredible, inspirational and literally insightful. It taught me that even through pain and sadness, we can still rise. The God that we praise on mountain tops is still the same God even in the valley and Liverpool seems to know this as a principle more than most Christians.

Irrespective of how many fights you have lost, the battle is yours for the winning. I do not walk alone. You do not, either. Shame, guilt, pain and anxiety should never affect us, maybe temporarily but we must be reminded of the God we serve. He does not condemn us so why should we condemn ourselves? We shouldn't! Liverpool Football Club went through many losses but they came out victorious, as winners. God can move mountains and calm the seas for you too, if you have faith in Him.

7. My faith

I know a lot of people who have named their children 'Faith'. It's a beautiful name and I hope those people really understand what it is to have faith and live a faithful life.

Faith is defined as believing in the unforeseen. My team and I prayed for Riverside Education and we believed that we had received it, even before it had physically manifested. We believed that we were going to bless other families and that our story would inspire others. We praised God and thanked Him for His mercy and provision. This was all in advance. As we believed God, He showed up in all of His glory. Nonetheless, we know that God has far superior plans for us all ahead, both collectively and individually. We know the God we serve so we are ready to serve Him and glorify His name. We await His continuous works which enable our lights to shine so that others, and even us, will marvel us all.

I have always believed that something gifted by God will not fail. Kupa, as his name suggests, is a gift from God. Some people may see him as a disabled young man and feel sorry for him but he is blessed, he is a free spirit. He has no worries and no pain. God appointed me and Molly as his guardians and along the way, He has given us the knowledge and ability to look after him. Molly and I have been able to bless many other families in and around Birmingham through our work with the school.

What an incredible God: He likes to use the most unexpected people, objects and situations to glorify His work. He used five loaves of bread and two fish to feed thousands of people. In the same way, God is using my son, Kupa, to expand the services of Riverside Education to bless other families in Birmingham.

8. Black lives matter

Concerning the current phenomenon of Black Lives Matter, I am very much a supporter of the movement and its original idea. I also believe that all lives matter too. God is love and He is just. As our creator, God wants us to love each other despite our colour or background. When Jesus was nailed to the cross, He didn't die for one race, He died for us all. The Bible also stands for equality and fairness.

Some of my most potent and pivotal relationships have been with people who are Caucasian and non-believers. Nonetheless, the common ground which Tony and I shared was our belief in equality and fairness. My current mentor is of a Polish origin and my two other mentors, who are pastors, are Caucasian too. This is the very reason as to why racism needs to be challenged and negated. Such relationships, with people who don't look like me or even share the same beliefs as me, gives me hope in a world which is an advocate of fairness and equality.

God has afforded me the privilege of seeing things differently and I have tested and enjoyed the goodness of being around people of various ethnic backgrounds. It is beautiful and full of lessons.

9. Love and hatred

When I co-founded Riverside Education, it was not as easy as it looks now. It was hard work. For the first time in my life, I learnt that I had actual enemies. I had people who didn't want the project to be successful and they let their intentions be made known. Once, someone had taught me: the moment you realise your purpose on earth and begin your journey to manifest it, the devil will start a huge fight against you. However, when you don't have challenges or elements fighting against your purpose, let that be a sign that you are walking in a purpose which is not powerful enough to shake the earth.

The devil targets those who cause havoc in his kingdom. He fights those who want to do well, for God's glory. I had become that person; still, God will send His angels to fight for you. He did that for me. With Tony by my side and so many other marvellous people walking besides, behind and in front of me, I was strengthened; I remain strengthened by the solidarity shown by both strangers and friends. The strength which God gave me also superseded every negativity which presented itself. The promises of God remind us that we shall run and not grow weary (Isaiah 40:31).

I discovered that there is a fine line between love and hatred. Though this seems and sounds bizarre, they are almost similar. When you hate someone, you think and talk about them all the time. You invest a lot of time in them, even if it is negatively, and in a bizarre way, you want to see them and know what they are doing all the time; there is a strange sort of infatuation. Do not be fooled, the same attitudes can be attributed to love: when you love someone, the only difference is the positive emotions you invest. Hatred kills you from inside but love heals you. Nelson Mandela was once quoted as saying hatred is like drinking poison hoping that the person you don't like will die. Hatred will kill you instead of the person you hate. God himself is love.

I decided to choose love every time I have a conflict with someone. Love is very powerful especially if you give it in the form of kindness. I use this a lot with my students and staff. When we have a situation that comes across as a disagreement, I always choose to offer love and kindness. It takes them by surprise and it works all the time because God is love. The way you feel about the person you hate destroys you and the way you feel about the person you love, uplifts you and makes you feel better. God wants us to love one another because there is healing in love.

I have prayed for my enemies relentlessly, so I grew full of love for them. God wants us to pray for our enemies and though initially I found this very difficult, I did it as a trial. During the trial, I saw miracles so I continued to pray for those who made themselves an enemy of mine. I continued to trust in God. Together, both my wife and I prayed for those who were against Riverside. Our hearts are at peace and God continues to be glorified by our submission to His will. The battles are His and the victory is His too.

God did not let us down because God never fails. He has fought our battles from the first day without us even recognising it. He has silenced our enemies and took the vision and the manifestation of it from glory to glory. The more our enemies tried to spread rumours about Riverside and even made personal attacks on us, the more the rumours turned into positive marketing and our characters were proven pure.

The unsolicited rumours became such an effective tool for marketing that we didn't even need a flyer to advertise Riverside's services. Molly once joked that it was like throwing a frog in a pond in the hope that it would drown and die but the pond became its natural habitat. What people meant for evil, God truly turned it around because in the midst of people attempting to sow discord, my family and I have learnt to lean on God whilst God has taught us how to make a natural habitat out of what the enemy brings. Riverside has been our natural habitat for the past five years.

Today, Riverside is in a very good place which is partly because of some of words and actions of the enemies of Riverside. Molly and I do not feel that we have enemies anymore but we have reminders from God on who is in charge of the whole project. We are aware that jealousy, hatred and malicious rumours will always be there but they will serve a good purpose for Riverside. Tony always tells me 'Abide, look at it this way, if you are doing everything well with honesty and integrity, you have nothing to be worried about'. This is how God speaks to me. He brings good people around all the time.

10. How to listen to God's voice

I decided to tell my story because God told me to do so. I don't know what else He has in store for this story or even how He will use it but I will wait for further instructions, soon after its publication. It's not easy to listen to God's voice and to know that it's God talking to you. Therefore, I need to share with you how to listen to God's voice as I experienced it myself.

1. You will know it's God's voice when you feel different about the subject. In as much as you will feel uncomfortable about what God has revealed, He will confirm it's Him with a peace which surpasses all of your understanding (Philippians 4:7).
2. There will be confirmation: someone else will hear from God too, concerning the matter and they will come and tell you. A close friend of mine dreamt about Riverside and she came to tell me.
3. God will provide the resources and people who share the same vision and even more passion. No matter how big or small, no matter what you have or lack, continue to pray and trust God with the little that you have because He will enlarge your territory and bring the increase. (1 Corinthians 3:6–9).

4. God will prepare you for the journey but be mindful that often times, He prepares you on the journey too. Your preparation is a process but take joy in it, knowing that God cannot fail.

5. God will open the doors to things that you never had before.

6. You don't sleep. God continues to reveal strategies to you, concerning the vision. You are always working on it. You don't get tired because God sustains and strengthens you (Isaiah 40:31).

In my case, when I look back now, I tremble with both fear and excitement of how God spoke to me and I didn't even realise it until now. Please note that it doesn't have to be one thing, it can be a combination of a lot of things and it takes a long time, especially in my case. I only realised the full picture of what God wanted me to do in my early forties. Never too late according to God.

Now I see how all of these chapters were literal pieces to such an intricate jigsaw puzzle which God predestined me for, before the very foundations of the earth (Ephesians 1:4).

1. God prepared me for the journey with my son through my studies and my professional experience.

2. God sent my friend from Zimbabwe to encourage me to start the school and before he left, he said to me, "I want you to work on this one now." On the first day, I went to bed at 5am.

3. God provided the finances through Tony, a source and resource I never imagined.

4. Several of my friends and other professionals had asked me to open a school of my own three years before I had the courage to do it. I say courage but I can honestly say, it wasn't God's timing before I actually did it. Also, I lacked faith: I didn't believe them and even one of them had a dream but I still refused.

5. God made me very uncomfortable in the work environment which I was in, to the extent that I started dreading going to work for no reason.

6. God started surrounding me with people with the same passion as me and people who were ready to work for me for free.

11. The Covid 19 pandemic

Towards the end 2019 we started to hear the news coming from China that there was an outbreak of a deadly virus called Covid 19 or Corona Virus. There was not much information about it except that it was concentrated in the region/province of Wuhan, there was no cure nor vaccine for it. We did not take much notice of it thinking it was just like another Ebola. We thought it would be contained in China and would never reach the UK. I knew a few people and one close relative who actually lived in Wuhan who had warned us against the virus and not to be complacent. They were right, the virus quickly reached Europe and the UK. As a school, we were not ready for it. I was lucky to have been in touch with a colleague who ran an online school and a month before the lockdown, I had been introduced to an online learning platform called Google Classroom. A few months before that, I had met a salesperson who also told me about online learning and how we can utilise this in our school. In more ways than one, God was preparing me for the pandemic.

A lockdown was announced for the whole country as a result of the Covid 19 pandemic. There was a lot of fear and uncertainty caused by the lack of knowledge on how the virus could be managed. There new information and new guidelines almost every day. The high deathrates announced every day caused panic and confusion resulting in a lot of people suffering from mental health problems and a rise in reports of domestic violence. Those who lost their relatives to the pandemic could not bury them properly. The number of people at funerals was limited. Most patients died alone and no one knew when the pandemic and how the pandemic would end. Above all this, some people were either furloughed or lost their jobs.

Both myself and my wife were classed as key workers during the pandemic. This meant that our children had to be in school for us to go to work. This was a very good gesture from the government but we had challenges. I personally understood the plight of the head teachers at the height of the pandemic. They had to ensure that the school was safe for both staff and students. There were not enough guidelines on how to do this and the safest thing was to have as few children and staff in the school as possible. Unfortunately, such a move also put a lot of pressure on parents who were key workers like me causing stress and mental health issues.

I am sincerely grateful to my staff who made it easy by being complaint to all government guidelines that made the school safe. Throughout the first lockdown, we had no cases of infection in the school. This was God at work. Just like other leaders of schools, I was concerned that there were no clear guidelines of what we would do if at all there was an outbreak in the school and lives were lost. God hid us under His wing and protected us. We had a health and safety inspection specifically for Covid and passed with comments that we were doing above and beyond what was required.

Again, this was God's reassurance that we were doing the well to protect our students.

We lost a few relatives and friends during the pandemic. May their souls rest in eternal peace. God was with us, my wife and my other son, Kudzy caught the virus too at its height but they recovered within a week. We got vaccinated and by December 2020 I had published two academic papers in renowned journals. God never stopped asking me to work. We are forever grateful.

12. Looking after Kupa during the pandemic

Looking after Kupa during the pandemic was one of the challenges we had not anticipated. As I said before, the pandemic took everyone by surprise and even developed nations like America were caught unawares and unprepared. When the government requested that schools stay open for children of key workers and for those children with Education and Health Care Plans (EHCPs). Kupa qualified both with an EHCP and ourselves as keyworkers. However, Kupa didn't understand what was going on. He lives in his own happy bubble. He was just confused by the changes in his routine and that we kept him more indoors than usual. He took it very well and it made me think of how blessed he is that sometimes he doesn't have to worry about what's going on around him. We do the worrying for him. He went to school on most days during the pandemic and he was kept safe there. The school did a fantastic job to keep everyone safe. At times Kupa was frustrated by being kept indoors and when we went out to the park, we had to establish a routine for our walk which he struggled with at first. He still follows the same routine even after the relaxation the lockdown rules.

The biggest disruption was the closure of Kupa's respite care for six months during the pandemic. We kept him home and only managed to squeeze a weekend away to Wales when the rules were relaxed. When the respite care was opened in August, the rota was changed and Kupa was only allowed to stay for two nights. We understood the precautions taken by the home and that it was for his safety. However, because Kupa didn't know what was going on, he struggled.

When schools opened in September, Kupa was sent back home on the first day because he had a 'high temperature'. When I checked him myself, his temperature was fine. This was after the school had claimed that they took his temperature six times. He was asked to stay home for fourteen days. It was the most difficult time for him. He had never missed school and his attendance had always been one hundred percent. He was eventually allowed back after ten days but he didn't display any further symptoms. It made me realise that the high temperature could have been as a result of his jumper that he usually wears to school even if the weather is very hot. I don't know how hot it was on his bus but something must have gone wrong on his way to school. I just felt the school could have been more understanding by recognising that children like Kupa could have a high temperature as a result of many other things that are not Covid 19. I also understood why they were that cautious. No one wanted to take any chances.

Just to make sure that Kupa's temperature was not as a result of Covid 19 we ordered a test for him. Taking a test for Kupa was like a visit to the dentist. We were supposed to take swabs from his mouth and his nose. These are areas that Kupa hates being touched. It was very stressful for him to have something being pushed up his mouth worse still in his nose. He resisted it with all his might.

Kupa doesn't know how to protect himself from the virus. At the time of writing this chapter. The government was encouraging people to sanitise and wash hands regularly, wear masks and observe social distancing (Hands, face, space). These are all simple things that Kupa can't do. Kupa will never wear a mask or observe social distancing but we believe that God will look after him through the amazing care he gets from both his school and his respite care. 'Look at the birds of the air; they do not sow or reap or store away in barns, and yet your heavenly Father feeds them. Are you not much more valuable than they?' (Matthew 6 vs 26).

At the park with Kupa during the pandemic

Walking with Kupa for his daily exercise during the pandemic

13. Kupa's brother Kudzy

On a visit to the House of Parliament for an event organised by the Spurgeons, a charity organisation that helps siblings of children with disabilities, I quickly learned a lot about this group of young people. They are in a unique position; they are brave and resilient. My son, Kudzy is one of them. His full name is Mukudzeishe, meaning praise the Lord. I always question myself if we are doing the best for Kudzy as parents with all the attention we give to Kupa.

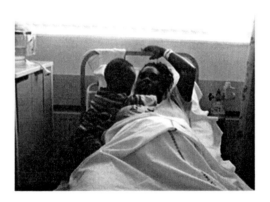

Kupa got really jealous when Kudzy was born. In this picture Kupa had visited his mum soon after the birth of Kudzy and he went straight to claim his place.

89

Kudzy was born two years after Kupa. A few months after his birth, Kupa stopped talking. Before this Kupa had been learning a few words such as papa, mama and even Kudzy, he used to call Kudzy 'baby'. At first, we thought he was upset and jealous of the attention we were giving Kudzy until his diagnosis of autism which also confirmed that it was normal to lose speech at that age. Kupa has never been able to say a single word ever since. Admittedly, we have always given more attention to Kupa for obvious reasons. I don't know how other parents cope with such a situation but I feel awful all the time. On many occasions, Kudzy has asked a few difficult questions such as:

1. Why does Kupa get away with things?
2. Why do you like Kupa more than me?
3. Why does Kupa not do work around the house like everyone?
4. What is wrong with him?

The two brothers can be as thick as thieves

Kudzy is very polite and well behaved and he is a typical 12-year-old but sometimes I feel he gets overwhelmed by what we go through every day. We try to answer the questions above as honestly as possible and make him understand how different Kupa is. One day he told his mother that he wishes his brother didn't have autism. He told her how much he wanted a sibling who can talk and play with him. As much as we can explain and encourage him to talk and play with Kupa, he knows it's different. He wants what others do with their brothers. It breaks my heart to see him talking to himself. He has actually developed a habit of having a full conversation with himself. There were times that Kudzy would imitate sounds made by Kupa and refuse to speak properly because he felt that was the right thing to do. Copying big brother.

Kudzy sometimes gets very angry and upset for no reason but we know it's due to his frustration of our situation. This usually happens when we cannot do certain activities, he likes because of Kupa's disability. One time we visited a trampoline place. I stayed with Kupa outside because he was upset, the customer services person refused Kudzy entry because he had to be with an adult. I went to explain my situation and he just said, 'Its policy, we can't help.'

It is not all doom and gloom though in our house. God has been faithful and constantly provides comfort. Praise be to the God and Father of our Lord Jesus Christ, the Father of compassion and the God of all comfort, who comforts us in all our troubles, so that we can comfort those in any trouble with the comfort we ourselves receive from God (2 Corinthians 1 vs 3). It melts my heart when I see Kudzy making an effort to speak to Kupa. He tries to do that a lot. Sometimes they play-fight and I see Kupa 'stealing' Kudzy's stuff with Kudzy in hot pursuit. When Kupa is away on respite, Kudzy says he misses him.

They have a proper sibling rivalry that is very funny. Kupa loves his food a lot and he always checks if Kudzy has been given more and winds up him a lot by eating very slowly so that when Kupa finishes his food he taunts him. It's very funny to watch. We are now beginning to have serious conversations with Kudzy about our plans for the future and what will happen to Kupa when he is older. Kudzy always says he wants to look after Kupa. That is very reassuring but we always tell him that's our job though we will appreciate the help.

We are praying that Kudzy continues to grow in his understanding of his brother. He is doing very well at school. He likes Art and Music. He is currently working on becoming a vlogger but his priorities change almost every day.

14. Conclusion

We have come to realise that all the material things we have are a blessing from God. He has trusted us with these riches so that we can bless others. Life has given us both oranges and lemons. We have been blessed enough to find a formula to make lemonade out of both. We recognise that whatever we are going through, however difficult it is, God is speaking and it is up to us to find his voice and follow his guidance.

We look at what has happened or is happening around us and learn too. I always think of people like Malala, the brave young girl who was shot point-blank by the Taliban and she ended up at one of the best universities in the world. She had to be shot first in order for her to go to that university. The people of Israel spent forty years in the desert before they reached the promised land. They had to pass through the desert to get to where they wanted. Both Barack and Michelle Obama suffered racism before they entered the white house and Jacob got his hip dislocated before he was blessed. We look at ourselves, with our situation and thank God that He is with us and we are here. We say Ebenezer.

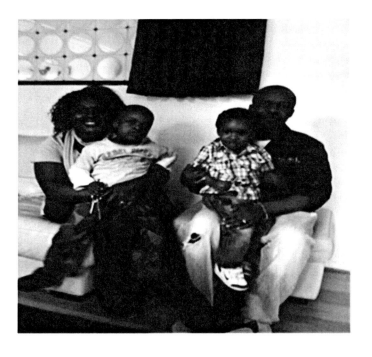

We are one happy family inspired by so many other people who have overcome their challenges.

15. Our prayer for you

Father, God, in the name of Jesus,

We come before you with a heart of gratitude and praise

Forgive us and help us to forgive those that we struggle to relate to every day

You are God yesterday, today and forever, you are God every day

You are God almighty, the king of the universe and author of salvation.

You are God on the mountain and you are God in the valley

We worship no other God but YOU, Alpha and Omega

We pray for those who are seeking you that they find you

We pray that the lost be found

We pray that the sick be healed

We pray that you comfort those who are mourning

Father God we thank you for your love

We thank you the gift of health and happiness and above all

We thank you for the things we have and those we don't have, for you know what's best for us

May your face shine upon all parents in the same situation as us

May your holy spirit be upon every person reading this book

May you bless all those professionals working with vulnerable children and help end the current pandemic we are in.

In the name of Jesus, we pray

AMEN